MANNHEIM STEAMROLLER

Impressions

By Chip Davis

ISBN 0-7935-4688-5

Published by

DOTS AND LINES, INK

9130 MORMON BRIDGE ROAD OMAHA, NEBRASKA 68152 402.457.4341

EXCLUSIVELY DISTRIBUTED BY

HAL•LEONARD® CORPORATION

7777 W. BLUEMOUND RD. P.O. BOX 13819 MILWAUKEE, WI 53213

PIANO SOLO
MANNHEIM STEAMROLLER
Impressions
By Chip Davis

CONTENTS

THE CALL OF ST. HUBERT

Composed by
CHIP DAVIS

Hunter's march

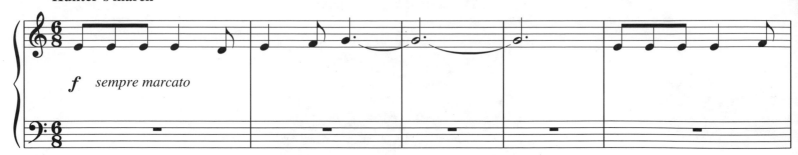

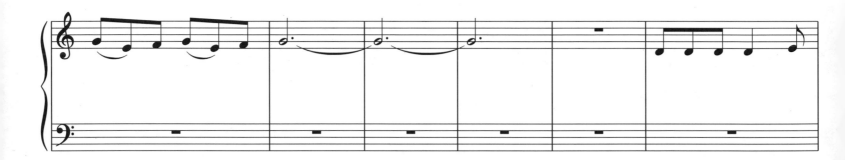

MIDI DIDI

Composed by
CHIP DAVIS

With a steady beat

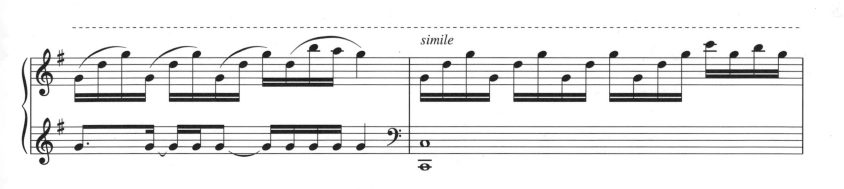

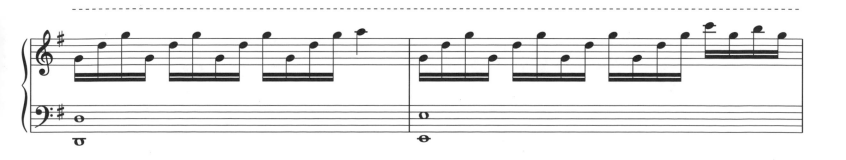

TEDDYS AND HEARTS

Composed by
CHIP DAVIS

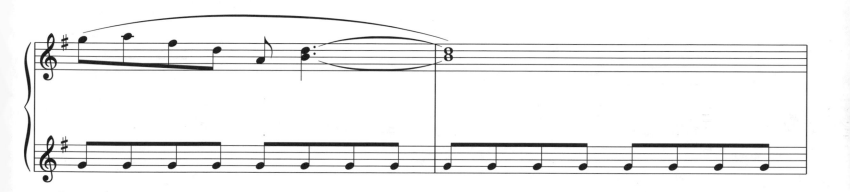

SERENITY

Composed by
CHIP DAVIS

molto rit.

CARRIE

Composed by
CHIP DAVIS

HAYIN'

Composed by
CHIP DAVIS

To Coda

THE BIRD AND THE BEE

Composed by
CHIP DAVIS

Airy and with motion

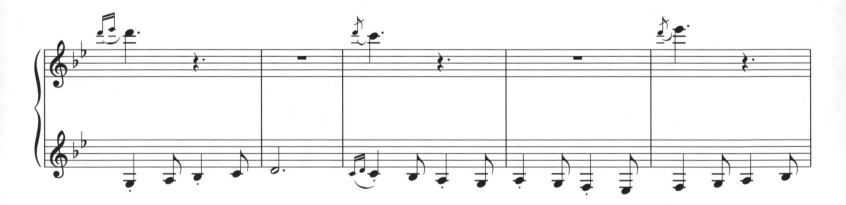

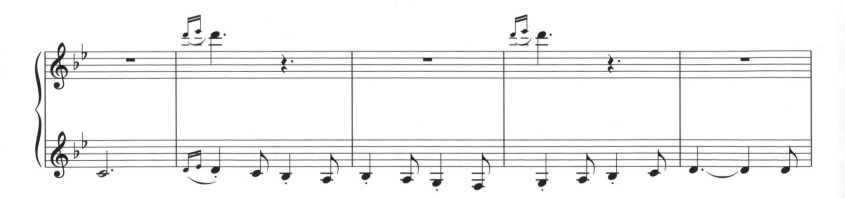

THE SIGN OF LOVE

Composed by
CHIP DAVIS

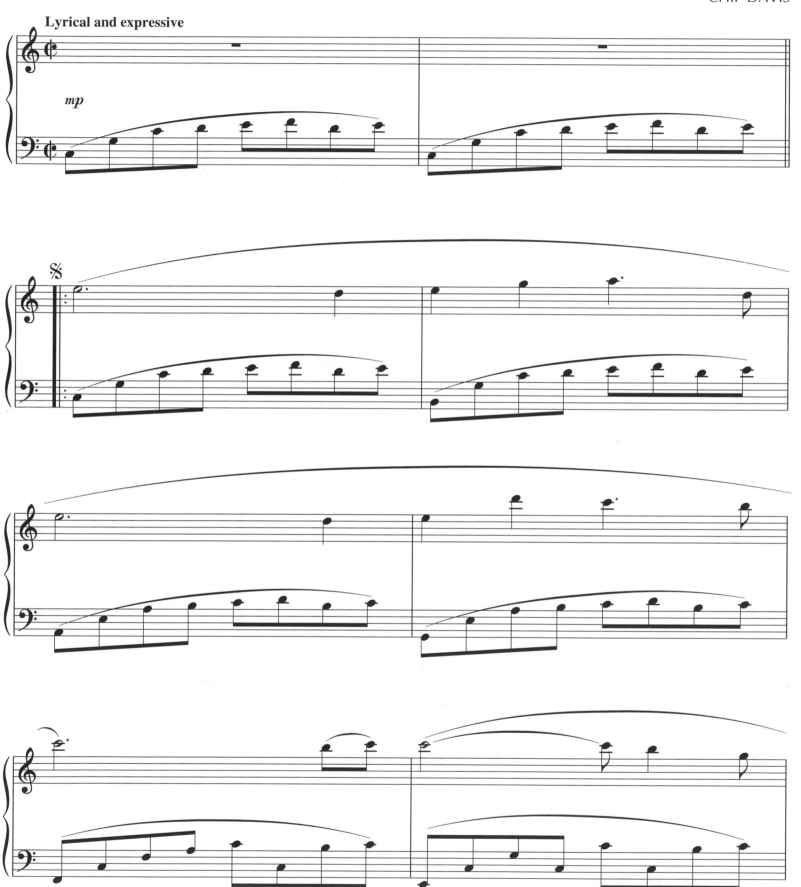

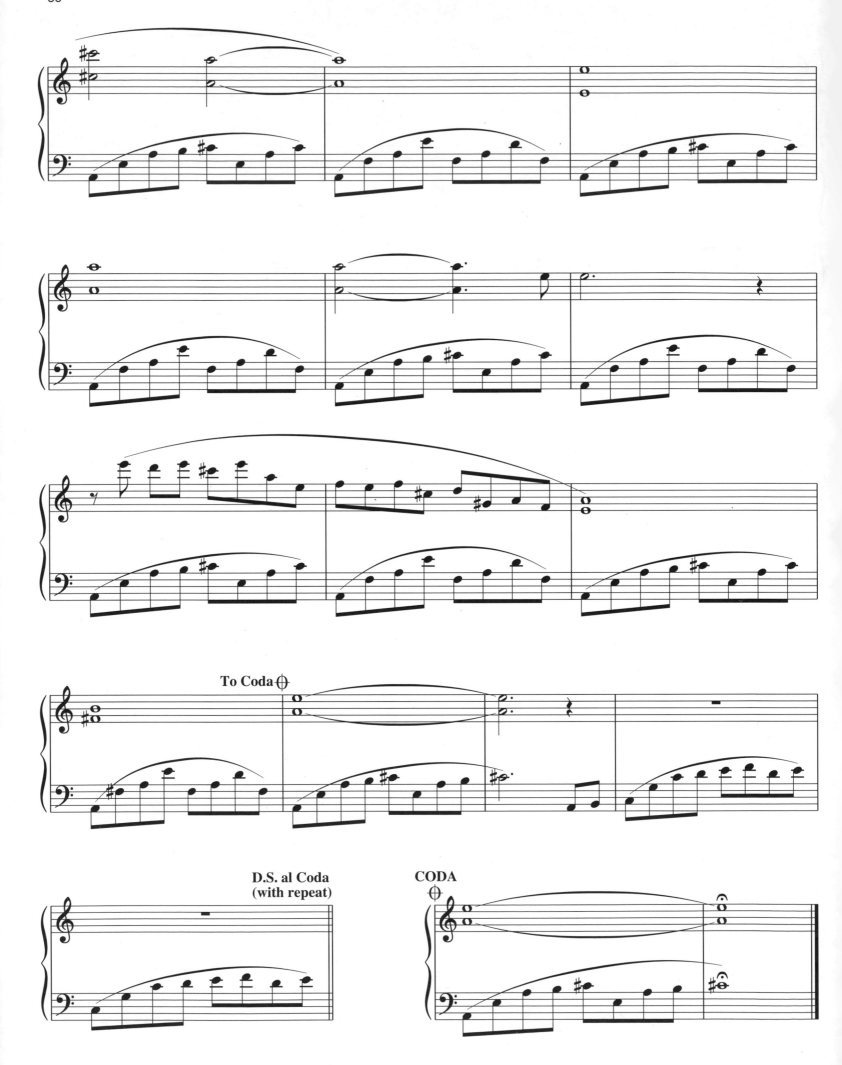

To Coda ⊕

D.S. al Coda
(with repeat)

CODA
⊕

A WINTER'S DAY

Composed by
CHIP DAVIS

Rather freely

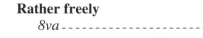

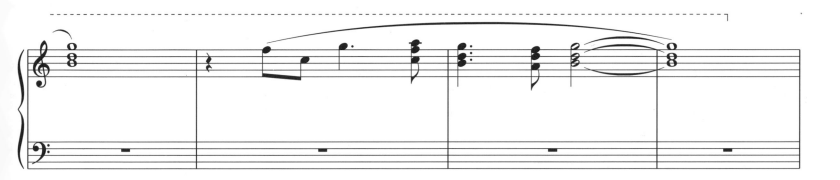

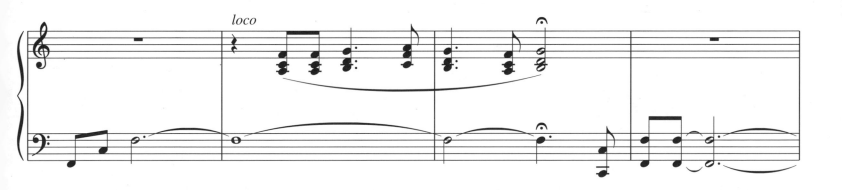

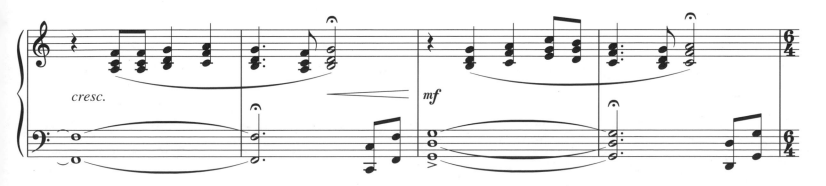

Evenly and flowing

mp

FIRST RING

Composed by
CHIP DAVIS

Freely

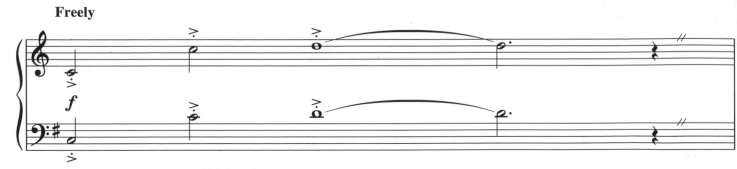

With pedal to create bell-like effect

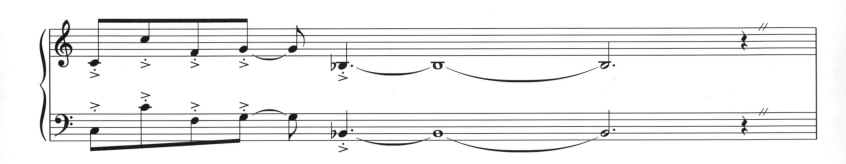

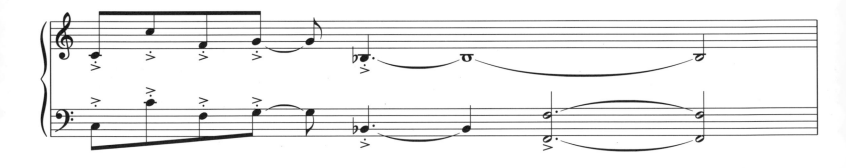

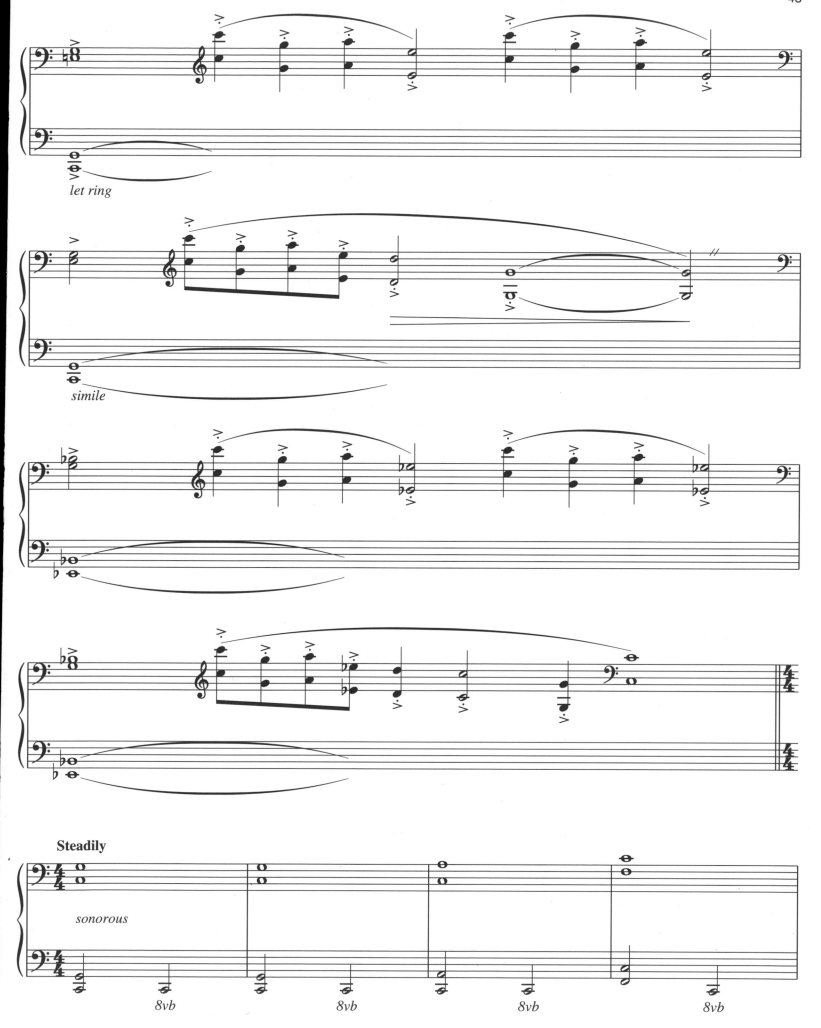

let ring

simile

Steadily

sonorous

8vb *8vb* *8vb* *8vb*

KALLISTA

Composed by
CHIP DAVIS

With a steady beat

Repeat and Fade

NATIONAL ANTHEM

Arranged by
CHIP DAVIS

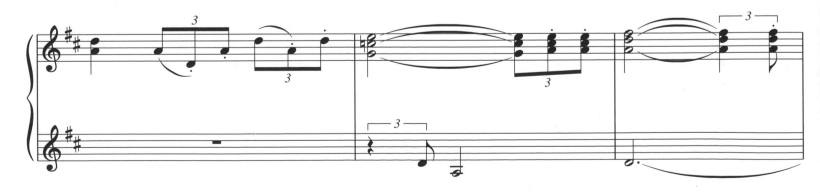

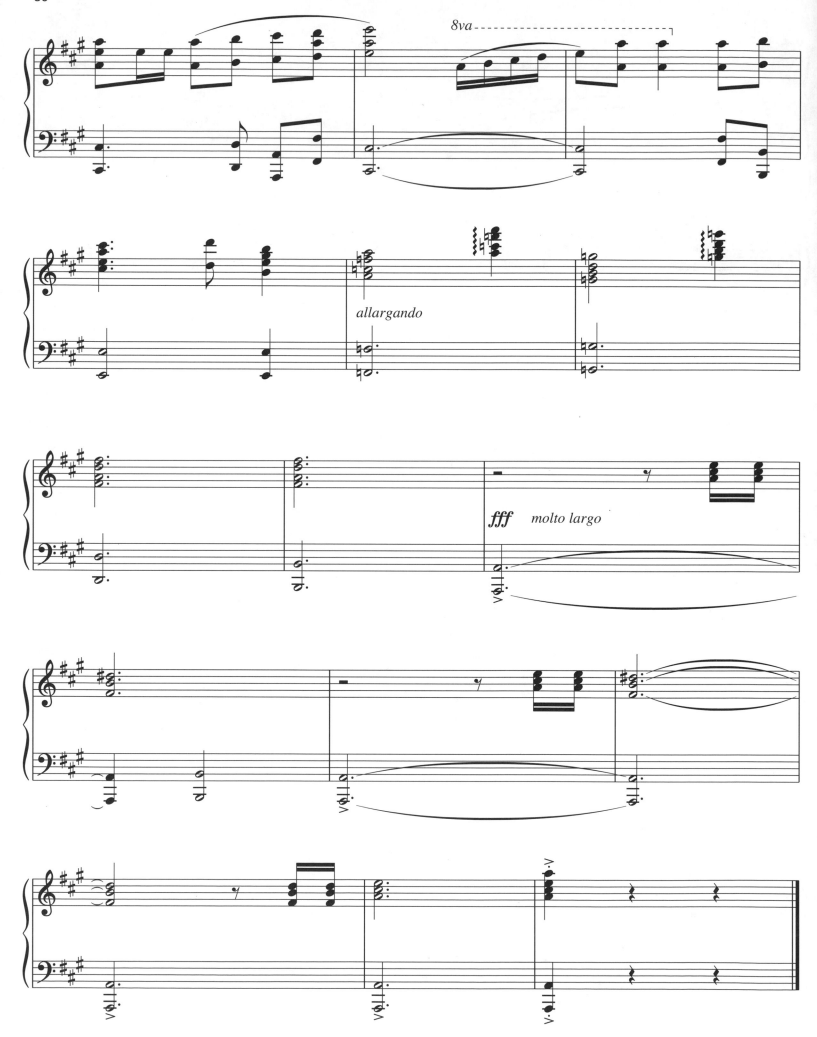

FUGUE

Composed by
CHIP DAVIS

Moderately

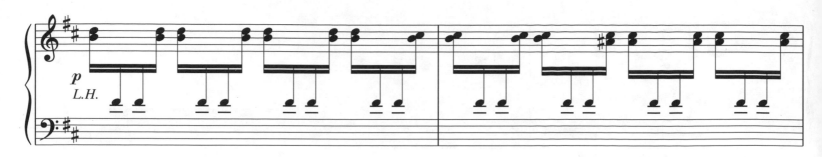

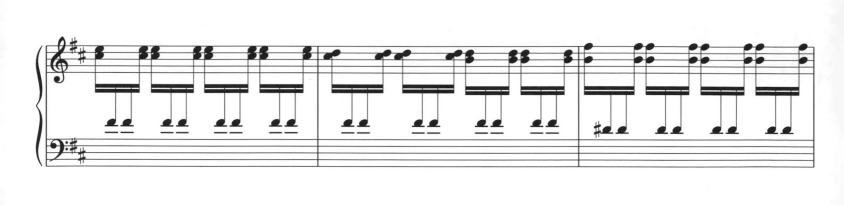

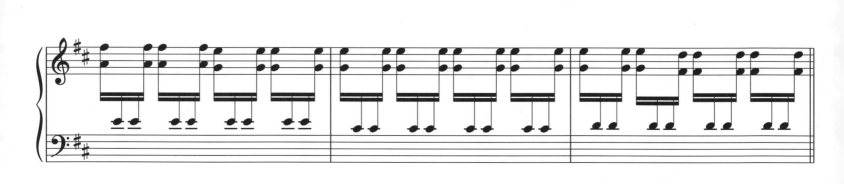

Play 3 times

COLORADO SPOONIN'

Composed by
CHIP DAVIS

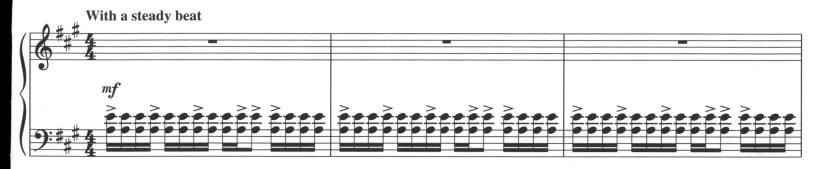

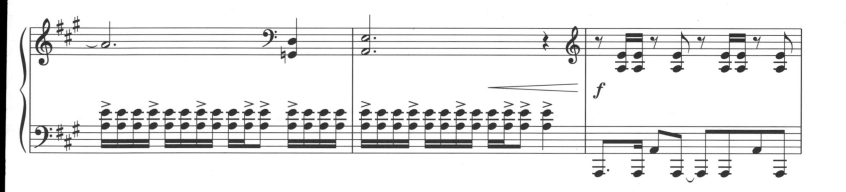

To Coda ⊕

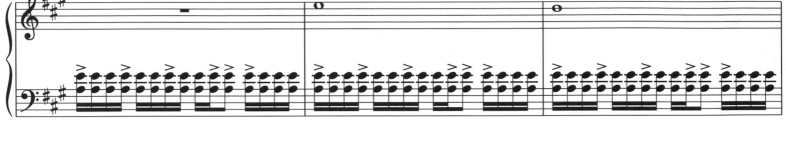

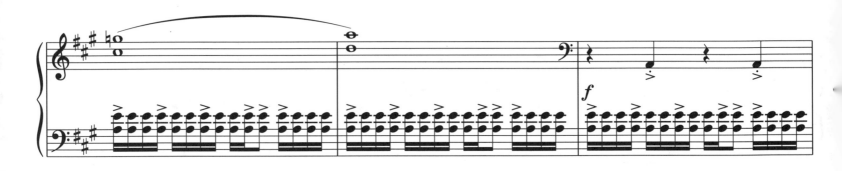

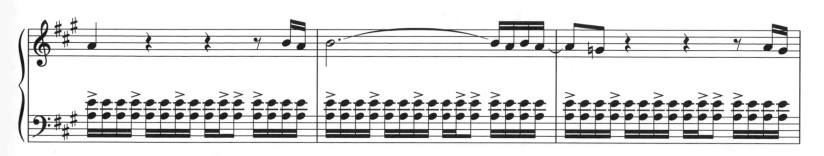

D.S. al Coda

CODA

MALIBU PEE WEE

Composed by
CHIP DAVIS

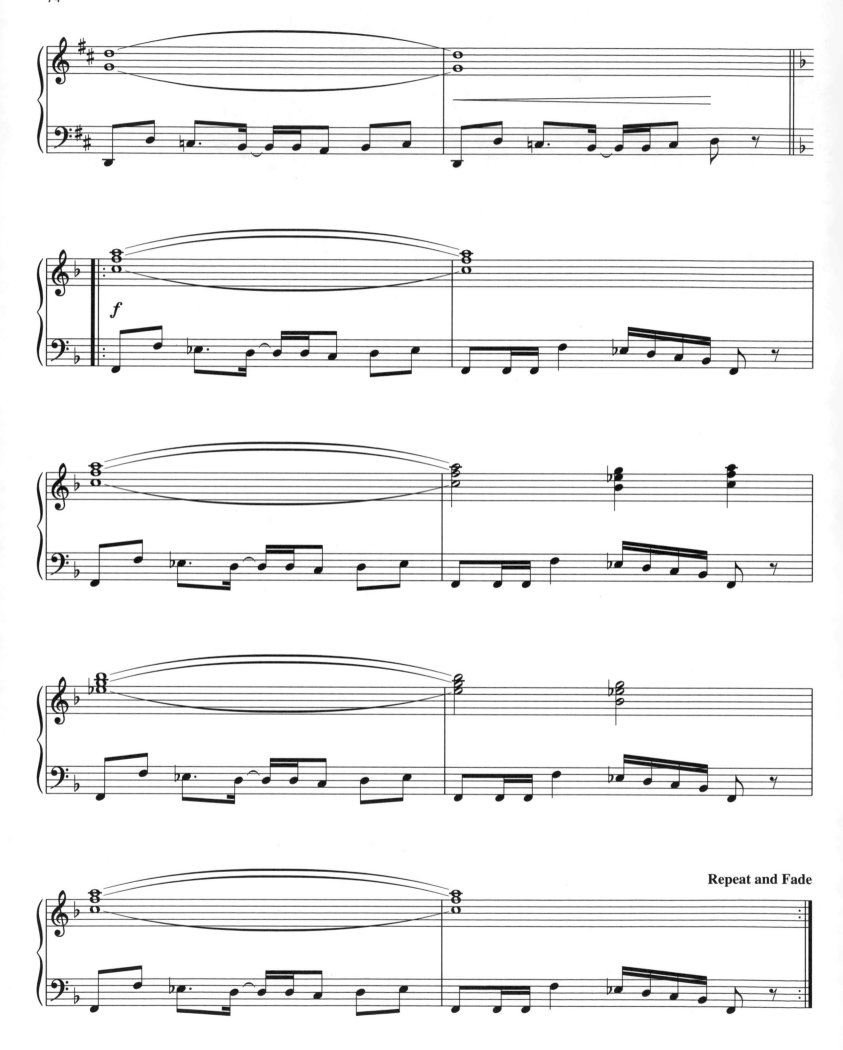

Repeat and Fade

AULD LANG SYNE

Composed by
CHIP DAVIS

Languidly

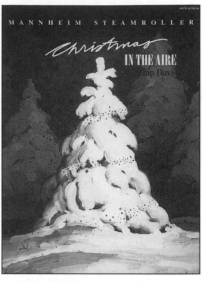